Steam, Soot & Rust
The Last Years of British Steam

Text and photography by Colin Garratt

Introduction

The 1960s

The following pages reflect a Britain which is no more as the 1960s saw the high tide of technology sweep over the remnants of the smoke stack age. The '60s were a time of moving forward with little sentiment for past traditions or what had gone before; a time when the word "heritage" had yet to be coined. And the railways suffered badly; some 40 per cent of the network was shut down whilst the trusty steam locomotive, with all its inbuilt simplicity and longevity, became the subject of a witch hunt and had to be disposed of as quickly as possible. The rich diversity of railway architecture also faced an uncertain future. If the magnificent Doric arch at Euston could be destroyed, anything was possible, as witness the serious threat to demolish the Grand Hotel at St. Pancras — a priceless neo Gothic edifice designed by Sir Gilbert Scott and one of London's most awe inspiring buildings.

Even the survival of the railway itself appeared uncertain in an age obsessed with motor cars and ever bigger lorries. Motorway building was rampant and global warming was another un-coined phrase. Harold Wilson's "white heat of technology" had little place for railways which were regarded by many as a leftover from Victorian times. They were losing money; they were comprised of decaying blackened infrastructure and were operated by smoke spewing kettles on wheels. Other heavy industries were declining too, industries which, like the railway, had made Britain the workshop of the world; ship building, ironstone mining, steel and coal. If the railway was to survive, an image of modernity was regarded as essential and in addition, working on steam locomotives was, by the 1960s, considered anti social in the blue collar revolution.

In this all pervasive mood, the steam locomotive, which had been Britain's greatest technological gift to mankind and the motive force of the Industrial Revolution, faced extinction in the land of its birth. That its disappearance broke millions of hearts was irrelevant. Also of no account was the fact that youngsters were deprived of that idyllic and worthy parallel to football — train spotting.

Although my interest is primarily with railways, the industrial landscape has always created an enormous fascination. I vividly recall railway trips to the Black Country, Lancashire, Scotland and the South Wales valleys during the 1950s and witnessed at first hand the dying embers of the smoke stack age; I cycled through the infamous Gorbals in Glasgow, explored Clydeside and saw the landscape of Lowry at first hand, all bore the blackened marks of a revolution spent. There was a stark poignant beauty about the industrial scene; grimy manufactories, belching chimneys, slag tips, back-to-back terraced houses and miles of railway yards. And at night, industry never stopped. The dull thud of distant forges, the chattering of machinery, the wash of factory light and the clanking rhythms of a passing steam train all combined to ensure the night's vitality.

By the 1960s the blackened scars of the Industrial Revolution were considered a blight and socially unacceptable. A massive cleaning up operation was embarked upon; slag tips and chimneys were taken down; derelict structures razed and sites which were once hives of industry cleared to make way for multi-story tower blocks, car parks and ultimately supermarkets. If Lancashire could be made to look like Buckinghamshire so much the better.

No. 4079 *Pendennis Castle* climbs Gresford Bank with the *Birkenhead Flyer*, Saturday, 4 March 1967.

The photography

To my eternal regret, I never correlated the industrial landscape with the railway. My principal task was to document the last steam locomotives and this to me meant intensifying the subject by such elements as exhaust effects, fire, dramatic weather conditions, the veil of night and the myriad effects of sunlight, smoke and shadow. The wider landscape, with its multifarious architectural or industrial structures — often in all their decaying magnificence — was largely overlooked.

And it took many years as a photographer for me to become sufficiently aware, to reconcile the two and portray the steam train as a player on the stage amid the whole range of other elements. I also now appreciate that the steam locomotive was born and died in the industrial landscape and its portrayal within it is not only relevant, but highlights a whole social order, which is also disappearing. The industrial vistas portrayed by Lowry are all but extinct worldwide; they have disappeared from the face of the earth.

Another important aspect, which was deliberately ignored in many of the early pictures, was the presence of people. My intention as a pictorialist was to present a documentation of the locomotive and I thought, erroneously, that the presence of people would be a distraction — people would look at people! Today, all these deficiencies have been rectified — albeit on a foreign canvas — but to my dying day I will be aware of what has been missed.

However, I was aware of, and fascinated by, the tension which exists between industry and nature and successfully captured this vibrant phenomenon. One of the best examples of this genre is the giant tree at Pennyvenie Mine (page 67), the hip berries at Nassington (pages 28/29) and the buttercup fields at Lowca exchange sidings (pages 24/25).

The vast majority of pictures in this book date from the late 1960s as, in 1969, I turned professional to document The Last Steam Locomotives of the World. The raising of funds, especially for the earlier expeditions, was paramount and I began a strict edit of all the pictures I had taken to date and sold hundreds of "rejects". What I didn't appreciate was that

Bagnall 0-6-0ST *Enterprise* shunts at Preston Docks on Wednesday, 20 September 1967.

today's rejects are potentially tomorrow's masterpieces; ideas change; the world moves on; the environment is in a constant state of change — not least the railway — and a locomotive type, for example, which is common today can become imbibed with a ring of nostalgia in years to come.

Fortunately many of the pictures sold went to David Nicholls, a Leicester based collector who allowed me to buy back all the pictures I had sold and without his generous support this book would not have been possible. And his help is doubly relevant as this is the first colour book which we at Milepost 92 ½ — along with our colleagues Calow Craddock td — have exercised full artistic and production control, embracing

of the pictures and recreated the moment and the emotions of the time when the pictures were taken.

Many of the scenes in this book have never been published before. I had always thought of this period prior to my turning professional as being a kind of proving ground and once the expeditions began in earnest, a race against time on a global perspective meant that these early British pictures were overlooked. It has been a real joy — almost half a century later — to collate them into volume form and relive those years and the amazing adventures we had in making the pictures. Fortunately, some written records of this period have survived and I am able to present some contemporary essays to augment the pictures.

Industrial Heartlands

The Lambton System: The Lambton collieries were situated 5 miles south west of Sunderland on land owned by the Earl of Durham and as early as 1860 had 70 miles of railway track. After amalgamations, the company extended even further and became known as the Lambton, Hetton and Joicey Collieries. The company made a prolific use of 0-6-2Ts, including some ex-Taff Vale Railway examples. The powerful 0-6-2Ts worked coal trains to the Lambton staithes on the River Wear. Other motive power on the system included a stored tank engine dating back to 1846 whilst the system also supported a Lambton built 0-6-0 tender engine of 1877. This veteran was to become the last tender engine to work in British industrial service until withdrawal in 1966. Steam finished on the network in 1969.

The Cumberland Coalfield: Whitehaven's collieries were situated on the cliff tops and the coal they extracted was either exported from Whitehaven docks to Ireland, the Isle of Man, or transferred by British Rail to Workington Iron and Steel Works. In its final years the Cumberland coalfield was worked primarily by Hunslet Austerity 0-6-0STs — one of the great designs in British locomotive history. The Hunslet Austerities were introduced during the Second World War when the Ministry of Defence needed a locomotive for heavy shunting, which was capable of starting 1,100 tonne trains on level track; 500 tonnes on 1 in 100 or 300 tonnes on 1 in 50 and the Hunslet design, based on that builders' 50550 Class, was accepted. The first example was steamed on 1 January 1943 and 377 of them were produced for the War Department by six different builders between that year and 1947.

The cessation of hostilities in 1945 found Austerities spread far and wide across Europe and some were destined never to return to Britain. After 1947 the War Department began to dispose of them with a batch going to the LNER and classified J94. Many others found their way into industry, especially the National Coal Board where the type was to become a nationwide standard. The NCB continued to order new Austerities until as late as 1964, by which time the number built totalled 484 locomotives.

The Backworth System: This system, north of the River Tyne, was steam's last stronghold in the north east. These coalfields were the cradle of steam in the nineteenth century and it was appropriate that the Backworth System was operated primarily by locomotives built by Robert Stephenson and Hawthorn, the company founded by Robert Stephenson in 1833 as the world's first locomotive builder. Backworth is steeped in coalmining history and it was enthralling to sit around the eternally roaring fire in the depot restroom and listen to the older hands tell tales of locomotives past and present. Tales, when told by these hardened north-eastern men, assumed a poetic lore of the steam age. Many of their descriptive phrases were a mix of ethereality and earthiness (Page 88/89).

Corby Steel Works: Vast quantities of iron ore were revealed in the Corby area during the building of the Midland Railway's main line from Kettering to Manton. This discovery was to give rise to a vast industry. By the end of the century several quarries were in operation, all with their own railway systems connected with the main line. In 1910, two blast furnaces were built. The advent of the First World War led to an increase in operations with more quarries being opened and these grew into a fascinating network of lines with large tonnages of ore being conveyed to the blast furnaces of North Nottinghamshire and South Yorkshire. The decision was made to develop Corby, hitherto a sleepy village, into a new iron town — with 500 million tonnes of iron ore estimated to be at hand. The development of Corby during the great depression in the 1930s led to huge numbers of workers, particularly Scottish and Irish, walking to Corby for work. I was personally acquainted with one worker who walked there from Cornwall. By 1930, Corby's population had reached 1,500 and so avid was the development that this had risen to 50,000 by the late 1960s. Apart from a number of other quarry systems Corby Works Division was split into two operations; Pen Green provided the locomotives for the minerals division whilst the steel division had its own range of motive power, particularly characterised by Hawthorn Leslie built 0-6-0STs, which were decked in yellow livery for maximum visibility in the gloomy works confines.

Ashington: The Ashington Coal Company operated in Northumberland north of the river Wansbeck between the East Coast Main Line and the North Sea. Thirty-seven square miles in all — fourteen of which were under the sea. By the mid-1930s this highly productive complex was producing 3½ million tonnes of coal per year from five different collieries and during the great export days much of the coal was shipped away from Blyth for export. Ashington steam coal was also sent to many motive power depots throughout Britain. The busy system included workmen's passenger trains.

The rich railway history of Ashington has been wonderfully documented by Stoker Redfern, who spent the whole of his working life there. He was a truly wonderful guide during my visit to the system in 1967. He informed me that between 1880 and 1958 over seventy steam locomotives worked on the system of which twenty-eight were delivered new, thirty-six came second hand and ten were acquired on loan. This total involved forty different types from a wide variety of builders. He also told me that during the twentieth century over fifty different types of main line locomotives appeared on the metals of the Ashington Colliery Company, including on one occasion a Gresley A3 Pacific.

Doxfords Shipyard: Doxfords had been important Wearside shipbuilders since 1840 and they were the last industry to use crane tanks in Britain. All materials necessary for shipbuilding were delivered to Doxfords by rail and the crane tanks transferred them to the various prefabrication shops in the yard. The parts were then conveyed from the shops to the fitting out quays on the River Wear. Crane tanks had been in service at Doxfords since 1902 when five were delivered from Hawthorn Leslie. The increase in shipbuilding during the Second World War led to four further examples being delivered from Robert Stephenson and Hawthorn. As the pictures show, Doxfords was an exciting place to visit; the highly animated crane tanks performing their multifarious activities against a superb backdrop of heavy industry.

Nassington Ironstone: The attractive Northamptonshire village of Nassington, tucked away amid wooded farmland, was by 1970 host to Britain's last ironstone mine. Operations commenced here in 1939, commensurate with the outbreak of the Second World War. Two Hunslet Saddle Tanks were purchased to that company's standard 16in design. The engines were delightfully named *Jacks Green* and *Ring Haw* after two local copses. The exchange sidings were with the ex-London North Western Railway's Rugby to Peterborough line.
Originally a working overburden of 10 feet was envisaged but over the years this increased to 65 feet, involving the trains working in a deep gullet. Nassington's ore was 30 per cent iron in content but this rose to 45 per cent following local calcination. It was a wonderful place for photography with some wonderful characters among the train crews like Bill Evans who had driven *Ring Haw* since new and in 1969 was approaching his seventieth year. Sister engine *Jacks Green* had been driven by Jim Hopkins since new. Now all memories — the exhaust beats of the trains as they echoed through the woods on a warm summers' morning, the cries of game birds as they rose in front of the trains — no superficialities here, just a friendly rustic system and some wonderful photographs too.

Pennyvenie: A stud of Andrew Barclay locomotives worked over the old Dalmellington Iron Works system, latterly part of the West Ayr area of the NCB. The journey from Waterside exchange sidings up to Pennyvenie mine was 3½ miles and mounting the footplate I was greeted by the most friendly set of enginemen I have ever encountered. Our engine was No. 21, a 16in Andrew Barclay 0-4-0ST of 1949 and we were propelling a long rake of empty wagons over the tortuous grade to Pennyvenie. On reaching Minnivey mine our boiler pressure had dropped to 120lbs necessitating stopping for a blow up. The cry of Curlews floated down from the hillsides whilst the song of a Woodlark erupted nearby. Further bird song was curtailed by No. 21's safety valves lifting and we continued our way to Pennyvenie. The pugnacious little saddle tank bit into the grade with all the tenacity of a terrier leaving an acrid trail of black smoke, which spread out across the valley below. The 16in Barclays at Waterside were augmented by a 18in 0-6-0T known locally as *The Big Yin*. This powerful side tank arrived in the summer of 1913 from Andrew Barclay and was to spend almost sixty years working on the section from Waterside to Pennyvenie. All Waterside's engines had improvised tenders attached made from cut down wooden bodied wagons.

Polkemmet Colliery: This West Lothian colliery was one of the most exciting industrial locations in Britain as the loaded trains faced a formidable climb from the colliery to the British Rail exchange up on Polkemmet Moor — a fascinating area of bracken and heather covered wilderness surrounded by distant slag tips. Two locomotives were invariably required and they literally charged the bank in an all out assault. At the time of my visit the motive power on offer was superbly varied consisting of veteran 18in Andrew Barclay 0-6-0ST, No. 885 of 1900 piloting a Hunslet Austerity of 1943. Only two of these 18in Andrew Barclays were built and they were almost certainly the first 18in locomotives produced by that company. The veteran was transferred to Polkemmet from Calder Iron Works in 1934.
Polkemmet had a reputation for vintage locomotives and their roster included a Grant Richie 0-4-2ST of 1917. The company also had a reputation for fielding the grimiest locomotives on the Scottish coalfields.

Goldington Power Station: Goldington Power Station was one of the landmarks on the Midland Main Line; located in the flat landscape south of Bedford, it looked magnificent in afternoon light. Also in the same vista was the giant hangers at Cardington, where the ill—fated R101 airship was built in 1929.

One of Scotland's finest latter day steam suriviors was the superb 0-6-0T built by Hudswell Clarke of Leeds in 1909. The veteran remained active at Bedlay Colliery, Glenboig, until well into the 1960s.

The power station, which dates back to the 1950s, was located on the banks of the River Ouse, adjacent to the ex-LNWR Cambridge to Oxford line. Two standard Andrew Barclay 14in 0-4-0STs were delivered in 1954 as coal burners but were later converted to oil firing. At Goldington, I detected some sentiment for steam power and it transpired that the station superintendent's wife was a direct relative of Richard Trevithick and some of his possessions had passed into the superintendent's family. One of the locomotives bore the name *Richard Trevithick*.

The South Wales Coalfield: Throughout the 1960s the historic South Wales coalfield retained a fascinating stud of industrial locomotives. On the anthracite field in the west, Brynlliw Colliery had three Pecketts. This Bristol builder was celebrated for the refined appearance of their designs; ornate curvature often being augmented by copper capped chimneys and brass domes.

Another Bristol builder was Avonside and one of their delightful 0-4-0STs, named *Sir John*, worked at the Mountain Ash colliery in company with ex-Great Western 5700 Class 0-6-0PT No. 7754. This engine ended a long tradition of ex-main line locomotives being pensioned off to industry for a further lease of active life. Another 5700 Class 0-6-0PT, No. 9792, built in 1936, worked at Maerdy along with a powerful Peckett.

The ex-Great Western engine was renumbered Maerdy Colliery No. 4. At Hafod rhy nys Colliery the ubiquitous Hunslet Austerity could be found and although these brought an air of modernity their grimy attire, combined with the semi-derelict colliery, created a classic industrial scene. Steam leaked from the ailing locomotives contrasting with the begrimed valley whilst the skies of South Wales seemed perennially grey.

Merthyr Vale Colliery at Aberfan sported a splendid Andrew Barclay 0-6-0T of 1953 vintage and numbered 1 by the colliery.

St John's Colliery at Maesteg also operated Hunslet Austerities, one of which was named *Pamela* whilst Taly Wain had a 1951 built outside cylinder Andrew Barclay 0-6-0ST named *Illtyd*.

At Blaenavon, two Andrew Barclay 0-4-0STs survived at an open cast mine set amid otherwise barren hillsides. All that was left of this once thriving iron town where, at the end of the eighteenth century, the night skies glowed crimson from the world's first iron foundries — Blaenavon iron was destined to girdle the earth. The two diminutive locomotives still bore the names of the General Managers' daughters of the Edwardian period and occasionally the veterans still coloured Blaenavon's night skies with fire, so evoking memories of those halcyon days two centuries gone.

An Old Salt waits at the crossing gates in Poole on Saturday, 3 June 1967.

A SOUTHERN IDYLL

The following piece consists of extracts from an essay written upon the end of steam on the Southern in 1967.

"It was early afternoon when I sat down to lunch in a Salisbury tea shop; the building dated back to the fifteenth century and epitomised the traditional English tea shop, homely and alluringly decorative. Placed upon the tables were white cards informing customers of an enforced closure.

"It is with much sadness that Mr and Mrs J. R. Brown announce that owing to re-phasing of the New Street Chequer Development 'The Bay Tree' will be closing on Saturday October 28."

My sojourn in the Bay Tree on this last afternoon was a rather harrowing experience. Telegrams of sympathy had arrived from far and wide and local people were coming to pay their last respects to what many of them regarded as a sanctuary. Opposite to me sat an elderly lady writing a poem entitled 'The Perennial Bay Tree' which, later, she handed to the manageress for inclusion with the telegrams on the pay desk. I sat immersed in thought, thinking of the modern age relentlessly forging its way into the future and yesterday's simple pleasures which are inevitably slipping from our grasp.

This experience in the Bay Tree drew a sinister parallel to my purpose for being in Salisbury on that October day as, that morning, I had made a final retrospective visit to the Motive Power Depot where the last remnants of the Southern Region's steam fleet were lying derelict and waiting to be towed to breaker's yards. I had wandered for the last time amongst locomotives which had once meant so much to me, each one individually holding memories of past adventures. I sat recollecting my Southern experiences which began in the autumn of 1966 when, in view of the drastic reduction of steam traction in most other parts of Britain, I made the decision to record the final years of main line express passenger steam on the Southern.

Initially I chose the area around the pretty Hampshire village of Brockenhurst, situated at the edge of the New Forest and served by the main Waterloo to Weymouth line. The mornings were invariably warm and sunny; blackberries abounded in the adjacent hedges and the forest was turning into an auburn blaze. I remember on the first day the signals lifting for the London direction and minutes later the mournful whistle of a Bulleid Pacific resounded through the still forest striking an almost idyllic harmony with the low murmuring of the birds. I watched the plumes of white smoke rising above the trees contrasting so beautifully with the blue sky. With a leisurely stealth which was so characteristic of these engines the train approached. The engine's condition was immaculate and the soft pounding intensity of its three cylinders provided beautiful syncopation. I caught a quick glimpse of the engine's well-oiled motion and decorative wheels as the train went past; 34008 *Padstow*.

In the thick of the forest the line was the only relief from the density of the trees. I came to know the Southern Pacifics intimately and as the autumn lengthened, I learnt to love the forest too in all its many moods. The sunsets and the enveloping dampness of the evenings when the exhaust from the engines would hang in the air for minutes after the trains had passed. The sun would set in its full autumn glory directly behind the east bound trains and this was a favourite photographic feature (page 114/115). I leaned to know the forest on the rainy days too and these added a mystical air to the railway. The spells between trains were sometimes lengthy and here one could enjoy nature at its best. Small flowers abounded by the lineside, the forest ponies were to be seen as fearless of man as they were of the trains. Newts, lizards, snakes and toads became an everyday sight, not to mention the many species of butterflies, some of which were peculiar to the New Forest.

On the advance to winter I moved on to Bournemouth. The Bulleid Pacifics were superb subjects; their nameplates were the most beautiful in railway history. The larger Merchant Navies commemorated shipping lines whilst the Battle of Britain Light Pacifics were named after the squadrons, people and places connected with the Second World War along with the West Countries, which celebrated the beauty spots of South West England.

Late afternoons would invariably find me on Bournemouth station in time to see the *Bournemouth Belle* depart at 5.13 on its 108 mile run to London Waterloo. Prior to the *Belle's* arrival an air of affluence would descend upon the station as this lovely Pullman car train inevitably attracted the elite and the well heeled. At a few minutes after five a Merchant Navy would gracefully draw in the spotless rake of Pullmans with smoke swirling down over the waiting passengers.

Bournemouth shed at night made a perfect end to the days and in between taking advantage of the hospitalities offered by the yard foreman, I would watch and photograph the servicing of the engines as they came to the shed. Bournemouth MPD was remarkably small; fire raking, watering, coaling and turning of the engines all being done within a few yards of each other.

The spring of 1967 saw more diesels drafted onto the system, steam being due to end in June. There was still much to see, resulting in my further exploration westwards into the rolling Dorset countryside through which the line threaded its way to Weymouth. Wareham and Poole were delightful vantage points. West of Wool the racing ground down to Weymouth commenced and my recollections of No. 34037, *Clovelly*, with the Weymouth portion of the 08.35 from Waterloo served as a permanent memory of what speed these remarkably free-running engines could attain when opened up.

The holiday resort of Weymouth at the western extremity of the line also served as a port for the Channel Islands and a spur left the main line to run through to the docks. The Channel Islands boat trains took this route to avoid the main station.

A heavy gradient, in places as steep as 1 in 51, faces the up trains from Weymouth before the line plunges into the 1,360 yard long Wishing Well tunnel. The tunnel mouth lies deep in a cutting and was a Mecca for sound recording enthusiasts and here on still days one could hear the trains leaving Weymouth and audibly follow their progress as they stormed the bank. The staccato bark of the BR Standards provided a marked contrast with the almost cultured rasping of the Pacifics. Here the disturbances of photographic feet and voices were a perpetual provocation to the ardent recorders who would situate themselves like sentinels over the grassy banks. How the unconverted Pacifics blended with the soft Dorset landscape, their names perfecting the air of relaxation; *Bude, Exmouth, Bideford*.

A Sunday morning feature at Weymouth would be the Channel Islands fruit and vegetable trains. Steam worked as far as Westbury and when, one Saturday morning the depot foreman gave me the tip that unconverted Pacific No. 34102 *Lapford*, was to be on this turn the following day, I decided that a car chase as far as Yeovil could provide some good pictures. Despite mist and heavy rain, 09.30 on the Sunday morning found me at the mouth of Wishing Well tunnel in readiness for the great lady. Within minutes I was soaked to the skin. Then, in the morning stillness, I heard the Pacific pulling away from Weymouth. Slowly she slipped and wheezed her way up the tortuous grades to the tunnel, her apple green livery seemed lost forever under a thick coating of grime. She was but a shadow of her past. The irregularity of the valve settings releasing her exhaust in spasmodic bursts. It was almost a foregone conclusion that *Lapford* would fail the grade but unrelentingly the veteran perpetuated her attack as with plumes of steam oozing from the middle cylinder, she approached the tunnel mouth. Having secured the picture and with *Lapford* hammering her way into the depths of the tunnel, I made my way back to the remains of Upwey station where I had parked the car. Furiously I drove towards Dorchester where I intended to photograph the train again as it branched off the main line and onto the ex-Great Western section to Bristol along which *Lapford* would travel to Westbury. However, having topped the summit of the bank, the engine had obviously found its feet and showed me a clean pair of heels to Dorchester resulting in my failing to even catch sight of the train again. Here then was an enthusiast's paradise, set in the twilight of Britain's steam age and as the warmer days of 1967 came, droves of enthusiasts from all over Britain descended on the Southern system where, despite a continual reduction in steam diagrams and increasingly dirty engines lacking both name and number plates, the majesty of steam prevailed to the happiness and excitement of so many.

I remember the warm sunny days at Worting Junction, the divergence point for the Bournemouth and Exeter lines. Here, the extra traffic created by Salisbury engines working on the West of England route helped offset the diminishing Bournemouth section. The Salisbury Pacifics were maintained in impeccable condition in both their two un-rebuilt engines; No. 34006 *Bude* and 34057 *Biggin Hill*, along with the re-builds 34013 *Okehampton* and 34100 *Appledore*.

During June I walked the Bournemouth line westwards from Worting Junction to Micheldever. The beautiful Hampshire countryside was restored to its full summer beauty and combined with the warm summer days put one in a world apart from the pace and tension of modern life. On the approach to Micheldever the line runs through two 400 yard long tunnels and I was invited by a Permanent Way ganger to accompany him through both of these. The two tunnels are separated by a 250 yard long stretch of track bounded by insurmountable rock cuttings on either side. Here, with his assistance, I secured wonderful pictures both of the trains traversing the short open stretch and entering the tunnel mouths.

We were caught amidships in one of the tunnels by the 10.30 ex-Waterloo travelling at high speed and headed by Merchant Navy No. 35013 *Blue Funnel*. We dived into a protection cavity in the tunnel wall just as the train was entering from the eastern end. The engine's screaming whistle resounding off the brickwork with ear-splitting dimensions as, with terrifying noise and vibration, the train screamed

past us, bouncing red hot cinders around our feet. The lights from the coaches in the swirling smoke throwing ghostly shadows over the tunnel walls. Whilst waiting for the smoke to clear my spine tingled at the unmistakable sound of another Pacific approaching, this time on the up road as, again with whistle screaming and howling through the tunnels No. 34104 *Bere Alston*, slammed past us with an express for Waterloo, emitting the thickest cloud of smoke imaginable. I thought I had seen the steam locomotive in all its moods until this experience in the Micheldever tunnels.

After a visit to Salisbury later in the month and two further days at Weymouth, the dreaded last weekend of steam operation arrived. Bournemouth station was packed with enthusiasts. Steam workings were limited and hopes were centred on the ever faithful 08.30 ex-Waterloo and when the train arrived, headed by Merchant Navy No. 35023 *Holland Afrika Line*, it was heralded by cheers and shouts from all over the station. The policy of the Southern Region on that last weekend was to work the majority of the remaining steam fleet to either Weymouth or Salisbury depots for withdrawal from service and eventual despatch to breakers' yards.

By the afternoon Bournemouth shed was a hive of activity as engines were being despatched either "light" or in pairs for the final run to Weymouth. It was a field day for whistling. As No. 34093 *Saunton*, trundled out of the depot for the last time all available engines saluted her. The gruff honking of the diesels, the lighter pitched BR Standards and the clear tones of the Southern Pacifics blended in an affray which could be heard all over Bournemouth. By night most of the engines had gone and the depot was to close that weekend. That evening, with acute sadness, I witnessed the little farewell parties for the many staff to whom the end of the steam age meant departure from railway service.

Sunday morning found me in Weymouth where all engines had their fires dropped upon arrival and were run into the shed yard. Only one engine escaped the graveyard that day. Merchant Navy No. 35030 *Elder Dempster Lines*, summoned at the last moment to deputise for a failed diesel on the 20:07 express for Waterloo. The ease and splendour with which the engine lifted that heavy train up the grades away from Weymouth made a hideous mockery of the whole situation. I was reminded of the last lines of *The Legend of Casey Jones*:

When the train go past,
when the train go past
Fellow take your hat off,
when the train go past

Perhaps the worst aspect of that weekend was still to come when, upon my arrival at Salisbury depot later that evening, I found the shed crammed full of engines, the majority of which had run down that day, many of them from Nine Elms. All fires had been dropped but the engines were still in steam and through the evening silence which hung over the depot could be sensed the traumatic presence of the condemned engines impregnating the air with that acrid aroma of oil and soot so peculiar to the steam locomotive. At the back of the shed stood two drivers talking.

I caught a fragment of their conversation above the gentle sigh of leaking steam from the dying engines; "Thank God they gone; we had a bloody cow last Friday night from Basingstoke, wouldn't steam, my mate were blacked up with it".

And so, with these reminiscences' heavy on my mind, I left the Bay Tree to commence the journey home to Leicestershire for the last time recalling as I went the words of *Macbeth*, act 2 scene 2, *'These deeds must not be thought after these ways; so it will make us mad"*.

Belgrave and Birstall station on the Great Central prior to closure in September 1966. Symptomatic of railway closures all over Britain the Great Central was the last main line to reach London which had opened as recently as the turn of the century and was a key through route for cross country workings. The line was built to continental loading gauge in anticipation of through services linking industrial cities of Great Britain with those of the continent via the Channel Tunnel upon which work had begun.

11

The Dying Embers

One story written at the time recounts a day trip to Lancashire on Sunday, 19 May 1968, some three months before the end of main line steam in Britain and a time when all surviving locomotives had been banished to Lancashire to eke out their final days. The essay reads: "Shortly after dawn we drove northwards through the sleepy suburbs of Leicester the only signs of life being a small group of anglers off for a days fishing. As we passed through the Peak District we saw the main line of the former Midland Railway linking London with the north conjuring memories of the graceful crimson locomotives which once blended so superbly with the countryside as to be almost part of it. The picturesque stations and the stone bridges echoed their memory with an air of solitude.

The first of the steam depots to be visited was Stockport but our anticipation was abruptly curtailed. As we made our way along the cinder track leading to the shed there were no spirals of smoke, no hissing steam, no sweet sooty smell on the breeze, only diesels. "Steam has been gone two weeks now" a fitter informed us; "a few got transferred, the rest all went to the breakers yard". Dismally we returned to the car leaving for the last time a depot which, over the years, had become so familiar.

Within a few miles at Tiviot Dale was Heaton Mersey depot, deriving its name from the river Mersey, which flowed alongside and over which we crossed to gain admittance to the shed. The utter silence told its own story; the depot had closed completely with the dieselisation of the area two weeks previously. Standing in ghost-like form were the engines, exactly where they had come in from their last duties. The atmosphere was acutely desolate; the Victorian architecture of the shed buildings and the gloomy shapes of the condemned engines seemed to defy the sunlight which crept in. It was as if the whole place was frozen under a spell.

However, the dereliction and feel of the place offered photographic potential and in a silence broken only by the murmurings of sparrows in the rafters we assembled our equipment. Among the themes made was a study of an 8Fs smoke box with an ornate gas light (page 72) and a theme through an old doorway featuring oil drums and the front of an 8F 2-8-0 (page 73) along with studies of the sunlight falling on the silent engines inside the shed. All pictures which capture the feeling of dereliction and dejection.

As large white clouds drifted across the early summer sky, we-crossed the Mersey and continued the journey northwards. The character of Lancashire revealed itself more with every mile and the great Victorian age seemed to have only just ended; a place where the past welled up to challenge consciousness of the present. Passing through Manchester,

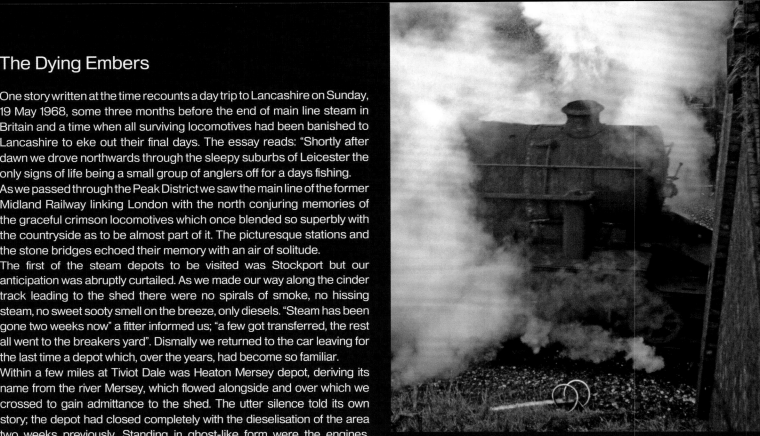

Above: A Stanier 8F passes a discarded street trolley, once a child's pride and joy, many of these were built from the chassis of prams but as the motor car began to fill the streets the children's trolleys became a hazard and began to disappear with them went the steam train another victim of the motor car. The example depicted here ended up — not uncharacteristically — at the bottom of an embankment where other items from yesterday's treasures could be found.

we arrived at Newton Heath depot, once famous for being the principal motive power depot of the Lancashire and Yorkshire Railway and also the place where Manchester United football team was founded. At last we were confronted with lines of smoking, hissing and gurgling engines. Despite the animation, it was obvious that the run-down was well under way and one picture I made there has become a great favourite. It is seen on page 87 and depicts two 8Fs visible inside the depot through a smashed window. It was not an easy picture to take as the window was too high to see through. Having procured a hand trolley to stand on, I found it was still not high enough and this necessitated shovelling ashes onto the trolley until the right height for the tripod was achieved.

Having enjoyed the animation of Newton Heath, we headed off towards the Eccles district of Manchester, to Patricroft where a further stud of live locomotives awaited our arrival. Here we were blessed with the sight of one of the massive 2-10-0 Standard 9F freight engines though, unfortunately, the engine was hemmed in at the back of the shed thereby rendering photography impossible. The engine had apparently worked in from Liverpool the previous week and had developed a fault resulting in withdrawal from service. In fine contrast, we found one of the only four named former LMS Black 5s, No. 45156 *Ayrshire Yeomanry*. I also made pictures of locomotives being coaled from the huge concrete tower which loomed high above the depot and the coal, falling down the chute into the engine's tenders, created a sound audible over a mile radius.

The last of the depots visited that day was Bolton which not only retained an active steam fleet but was noted for keeping it in spotless condition. Set in a sea of *Coronation Street* houses, Bolton Motive Power Depot was approached by traversing narrow streets across which hung lines of decorative and varied washing. These streets were never designed for the motor car. Getting out of the car, my companion dutifully lifted each of these high enough to enable me to drive underneath without incurring any wrath from the owner. Nevertheless, with each line one almost expected to see the face of Ena Sharples glowering at us through the well-polished windows.

We traversed the street without being confronted and entered the depot. It was now late afternoon and many of the engines were being lit up for the new week's workings as they were diagrammed to leave the shed in the early hours of Monday morning. The smoke oozing up through the roof vents formed a grimy pall, which hung high over the depot and could be seen all over the town. Here again there was much to set down on film. Light repairs were still being undertaken in a small bay attached to the shed. Fitters working with carbide lamps on the valve gear made fascinating pictures. Time was now running short and with the gathering dusk came a steady rain. Out on the main line a Black 5 stood starkly against the darkening sky, contrasting beautifully with the Lancastrian backdrop of slate roofs and factory chimneys. A pall of steam and smoke rose from the engine as, in the thickening gloom, the lights of the houses began to appear, the atmosphere heightened and the scene acquired a rare depth.

As we made our way homewards through the driving rain we seemed to be returning from a dream land, a land of giants which spat fire; a strange and wonderful land of elemental forces which no longer had any place in our reality. On to the motorway, back into the present; soon another car was lost amid the spray on the southbound carriageway.

Colin Garratt, complete with Weston V light meter, at Springs Branch shed, Wigan, on Tuesday, 19 September 1967.

Right: The end of the steam age in industrial Lancashire.

Opposite page, top left: Lostock Hall Depot in Preston with Ivatt 2-6-0 No. 43046.

Opposite page, top right: Trafford Park Shed with Stanier 8F No. 48535 on 18 September 1967.

Opposite page, bottom: Carlisle Upperby with BR Standard 4 No. 75019, derelict, 23 September 1967.

Condemed Stanier 8F 2-8-0s at Patricroft depot waiting to be towed away to breakers yards.

Above: Stafford Motive Power Depot.

Nature quickly gains supremacy at Stafford and Bedford motive power depots, the former from the London & North Western Railway West Coast Main Line and the latter from the

Loading ironstone and slewing track on the Corby Minerals Division network in 1968

Nassington's two 16in Hunslet 0-6-0STs wait for their wagons to be filled at the working face in the gullet, 1969.

A loaded ironstone train heads through the gullet at Nassington past seams of outcropping silica white sand.

On Saturday, 3 June 1967, ex-LNER A4 Class Pacific No. 4498 *Sir Nigel Gresley* worked an enthusiast's special from London Waterloo to Bournemouth. The thoroughbred is seen here bringing the empty stock up to Bournemouth Central from Branksome Carriage Sidings for the return journey to London.

BR Standard 5 Class 4-6-0 No. 73085, a Nine Elms engine, heads westwards through the flowery cuttings between Bournemouth and Poole with an afternoon train for Weymouth. Saturday, 3 June 1967.

Hunslet Austerity 0-6-0STs in NCB service on the Cumberland coalfield. These classic war engines were introduced in 1943 as a design for the War Department and seven different builders were involved in their construction.

On the cliff tops above Whitehaven.

This picture below shows one of the Cumberland Coalfield's Giesl fitted Austerities permeating the meadows at the exchange siding with the selfless aroma of coal smoke.

Above: The final working of the 00.55 Carnforth — Burnley freight, leaving Carnforth Midland
yard on Saturday, 3 August 1968. Complete with smoke ring.

Left: Carnforth shed yard, August 1968.

Hip berries at Nassington Ironstone with the system's 16in Hunslet 0-6-0STs named *Jacks Green* and *Ring Haw* after two local coppices.

If you were to walk down the gangways past the lines of silent locomotives and go through that doorway at the far end of the shed you would find more engines outside rusting away amid weed covered yards.

Mottles at Patricroft, summer 1968. This depot was one of Britain's most important and its closure in 1968 left lines of Stanier 8F 2-8-0s, Black 5 4-6-0s and BR Standard 5 4-6-0s — some with Caprotti valve gear and only a few years old. They lay amid the silenced depot prior to being hauled away to breakers yards the halcyon days of Patricroft's "rare Jubilees" having passed. Some of the 8Fs in these scenes were destined for Cohens Scrapyard near Kettering, a site on the former Loddington Ironstone branch set aside for breaking up locomotives.

Above: Sunrise on the Backworth Colliery network north of the River Tyne finds a Hunslet Austerity 0-6-0ST hauling a loaded train from the washery at Fenwick.

Opposite page, top: A Hunslet Austerity 0-6-0T on the Whittle Colliery system in Northumberland.

Opposite page, bottom: A watery dawn at Pen Green on the mineral division of Corby iron and steel works revealing a brace of 0-6-0 saddle tanks based on an earlier design of Kitson of Leeds.

Right: Staithes and winding gear on the Lambton System.

Right: Hunslet Austerity on the Backworth System.

Opposite page, top left: Yorkshire Engine Company 0-6-0ST at Clipston Colliery, Nottinghamshire.

Opposite page, top right: Ex-Great Western 0-6-0PT at Mountain Ash Colliery.

Opposite page, below: Andrew Barclay 0-6-0T at Merthyr Vale Colliery, Aberfan.

Above: Fireman Walker at the regulator of Stanier 8F No. 48257.

Top right: Depot steam raiser whose job, like the locomotives themselves, will be swept into history.

Right: Steam raiser lighting fire in Bournemouth locomotive depot, 1967.

Above: A locomotive fitter complete with hammer and carbide lamp. Rose Grove depot, Burnley on Tuesday, 18 June 1968.

Left: A fitter complete with oil lamp and hammer undertakes a repair to an ex-LMS Stanier 8F Class 2-8-0 at Rose Grove depot, Burnley on Tuesday, 18 June 1968.

Artisans par excellence:

Above: Locomotive fitters.

Right: Locomotive fitters at Wigan Springs branch.

Left: A Shedman applies spit and polish at Salsbury depot to the nameplate of rebuilt Bulleid Pacific No. 34040 *Crew Kerne*.

Below: End of shift, cycles at the ready. How L. S. Lowry would have painted the gaunt building in the background — already conjuring up its own foggy aura.

41

Rebuilt West Country Pacific No. 34004 *Yeovil* at Bournemouth MPD.

Above: West Country No. 340
at Salisbury in its home shed. T
running unrebuilt Bulleid Pacif
broken up by Cashmores of N
September 1967.

Left: BR Standard 4 No. 75074
Bournemouth with Merchant N
No. 35030 *Elder Dempster Li*

Stephenson and Hawthorn 0-4-0ST
er Power Station.

Drama at Cadley Hill Colliery on the Derbyshire coalfield with *Empress* a 16in 0-6-0ST introduced as a standard design by Bagnalls of Stafford in 1944.

A definitive overcast day complete with rainstorm as unrebuilt Bulleid Pacific No. 34002 *Salisbury*, receives the green light at Basingstoke at the head of a stopping train to Waterloo on 27 December 1966. The wet gloomy day did not discourage the grandfather from taking his grandson for an unforgettable afternoon watching the trains. The engines forlorn appearance and leaking steam suggested early withdrawal and *Salisbury* was destined to be taken out of service several months later and broken up at Cashmores, Newport.

The rain beats down unremittingly as Bulleid Pacific No. 34052 *Lord Dowding* arrives at Basingstoke at the head of a semi-fast from London Waterloo. Saturday, 24 December 1966.

Doxford crane tanks at work in Pallion shipyard on the River Wear in Sunderland. The Sunderland Echo of Friday, 18 December 1970 carried a heading "The old Pallion yard workhorses to retire" and thus heralded the end of an important tradition in British locomotive history. The heading referred to the last working crane tanks in the country which were to cease duty at Doxford's Shipyard in Pallion, Sunderland, on 29 January 1971.

Crane tanks originated in the second half of the last century and were employed both in the works of main-line companies and in heavy industry where bulky and awkwardly shaped loads had to be handled.

A vessel takes shape in the fitting out berth at Doxford's Pallion Shipyard on the River Wear in Sunderland. One of the company's 0-4-0CT delivers sections to the fitting out berths.

Above: With a banker attached, a Stanier 8F climbs Shap during a rain storm on 27 September 1967.

Opposite page: The view from the banker in the form of a BR Standard 4-6-0.

Above: Rolling stock stabled at Ashington Colliery including pre-grouping ex-main line coaches once used for the system's dense workmen's passenger services. Monday, 25 September 1967.

Below: Ashington atmosphere with an 18in Robert Stephenson and Hawthorn 0-6-0ST (left) and a Hunslet Austerity (right). Monday, 25 September 1967.

Above: A Hunslet Austerity passes beneath an aerial ropeway on the Ashington Colliery system near Morpeth, 25 September 1967.

Left: A pair of 0-4-0STs bask amid the sunlight at Philadelphia Colliery County Durham on Friday, 22 September 1967.

Over page: Foggy day at Cranford on Northamptonshire ironstone, 28 November 1968.

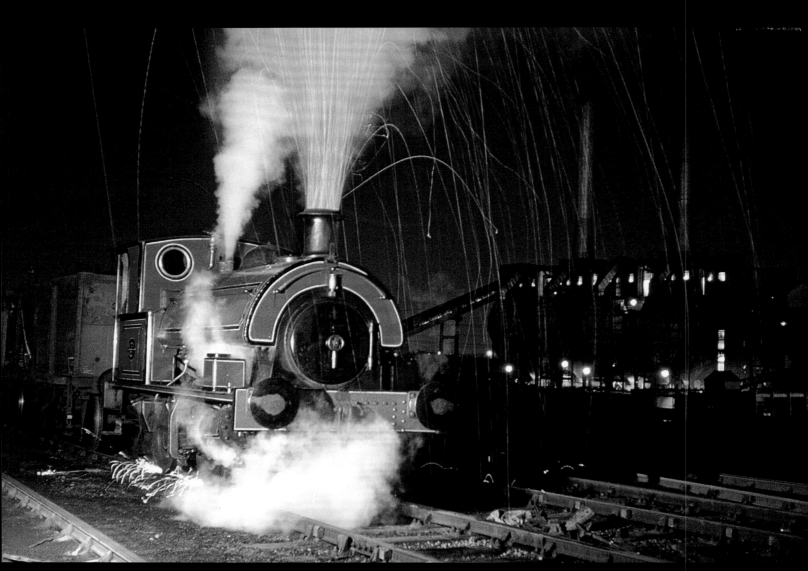

Above: Leicester Power Station, Raw Dykes Road, with their immaculate Robert Stephenson and Hawthorns 0-4-0ST.

Above: Clipstone Colliery, Nottinghamshire, with their Yorkshire Engine Company workhorse 0-6-0ST.
Built at the company's Meadowhall works in Sheffield.

A blustery autumn day at Goldington Power Station, south of Bedford, with Andrew Barclay 0-4-0ST ED No. 9 at work. Whilst at Goldington, I sensed a sympathetic approach to continue with steam traction, this was quite pronounced and I later learned that the superintendent's wife was a direct relative of Richard Trevithick and that some of his possessions had passed into her family. Consequently, one of the engines was named *Trevithick*. The two RSH 0-4-0STs in service at Goldington were both oil burners.

Ex-Great Western Railway Castle Class No. 7029 *Clun Castle* (actually built by BR) reposes at Tyseley shed whilst working special trains associated with the end of steam.

Another famous engine of the time was LNER A4 *Bittern* caught here at Leeds Holbeck roundhouse. *Bittern* was one of a batch of A4s which ended their days on express workings between Glasgow and Aberdeen.

Silent motion: studies in Walschaerts valve gear.

The heart and soul of a working steam locomotive is its valve gear and the most common in use all over the world is Walschaerts.
It provides a tapestry of rods which provide both movement and fascination.

Andrew Barclay engines at work on
the Waterside network of the NCB's
West Ayr Division.

An 18in 0-6-0T of 1913 nicknamed
The Big Yin.

16in standard Andrew Barclay 0-4-0ST
No. 21, delivered to Waterside new in 1951.

Above: A Hunslet Austerity saddle tank works on the Shilbottle Colliery network near Alnwick.

Opposite page, top: A 17in Robert Stephenson and Hawthorns 0-6-0 ST heads across the Whittle Colliery network.

Opposite page, bottom: Whittle Colliery at Newton on the Moor operated this last surviving 18in 0-6-0T, built by Robert Stephenson and Hawthorns in 1950 and numbered 31. The locomotive is ex-Ashington, another view of

Former Great Western 5700 Class 0-6-0PT No. 9792 lies out of use at Maerdy Colliery. Built in 1930, this engine was re-numbered No. 4.

Thomas Muir's scrapyard at Easter Balbeggie in Fife with a turn of the century Andrew Barclay 0-4-0ST contrasting with an MG Magnette car.

Right: B1 at Low Moor.

Far right: 8F No. 48117 at Heaton Mersey depot on Sunday, 19 May 1968.

Right: Fairburn 2-6-4Ts at Wakefield on Saturday, 14 October 1967.

Barrels at Heaton Mersey on Sunday, 19 May 1968.

View from the cab interior of a condemned engine.

Opposite page: Bolton Motive Power Depot on
Sunday, 18 May 1968.

Left: Carnforth.

Left: Rose Grove.

Far left: Newton Heath.

Scenes following closure of the Market Harborough to Northampton line in 1973. This line was a last link in the main line workings of the ex-LNWR Super D 0-8-0s known as Weasers. During the 1950s seven of these engines were allocated to Leighton Buzzard for working sand trains from pits in the area — these classic heavy freight engines made a fine sight as they traversed the scenic section between Northampton and Market Harborough.

The line was opened in 1859 with eight stations and two tunnels and the one seen here is Oxendon, which is 462 yards long. The Northampton to Market Harborough line connected with the LNWR West Coast Main Line and the Midland Main Line at Market Harborough. Latter day passenger trains on the Market Harborough to Northampton line were sometimes powered by ex-LMS 2P 4-4-0s fitted with Dabeg water heaters.

Ladies of Blaenavon: A fine drama at Blaenavon one of the once great iron towns of the Industrial Revolution featured are two Andrew Barclay 0-4-0 saddle tanks which once belonged to the old Blaenavon Iron Company. They are *Toto* and *Nora* built at Andrew Barclay's Kilmarnock works in 1919 and 1920. *Toto* was the name of the old General Manager's dog, whilst *Nora* was named after one of his several daughters.

e and Cranford.

Contrast in departures a study of Bulleid Pacifics receiving the green light: Merchant Navy Class No. 35030 *Elder Dempster Lines* prepares to depart from Wareham with a Weymouth train. In contrast, one of the last surviving un-rebuilt West Country Pacifics No. 34102 *Lapford* receives the right of way from Bournemouth with a London-bound train.

End of steam specials, July and August 1968.

Right: North of Settle, two Black 5s head southwards with the final BR steam train from Carlisle to Liverpool on Sunday, 11 August.

Far right: Two Black 5s climb to Copey Hill summit on Sunday, 4 August.

Right: A brace of BR Standard 4s approach Skipton with a British Rail end of steam special on Sunday, 28 July.

Left: On the climb to Copey Hill summit near Todmorden with an end of steam special from Liverpool to Carlisle on Sunday, 4 August.

It is ironic that this official "end of steam" special should remind us that not everyone was sad to see steam go as witness the splendid line of washing. Throughout the steam age housewives all over the country had suffered spoilt washing.

Bottom right: BR Standard 4 No. 75019 seen through the roundhouse windows at Carlisle Upperby.

Below: BR Class 9F 2-10-0.

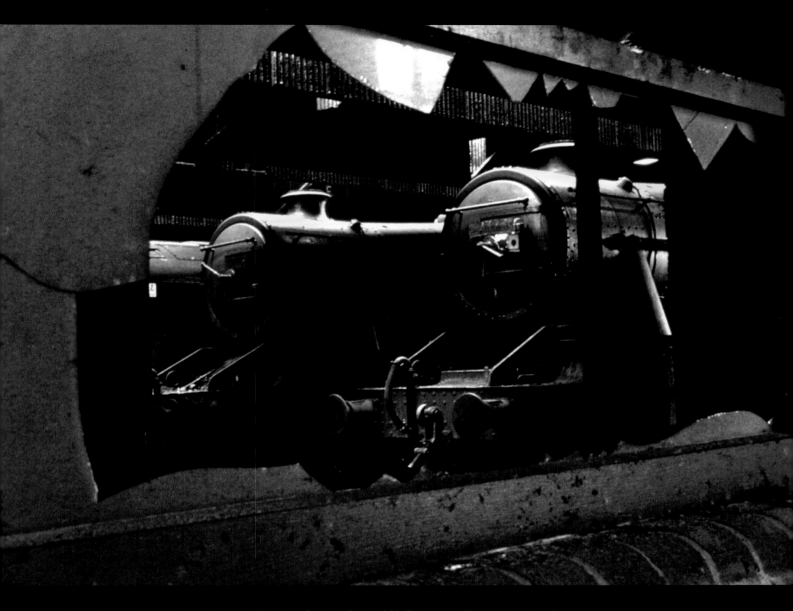

Above: Two ex-LMS 8Fs at Newton Heath Depot on Sunday, 19 May 1968. This was a difficult picture to make; the broken window that I wanted to use for a frame was some way above the ground, making it difficult to obtain a camera viewpoint. Something needed to be found on which to stand the camera tripod. A search of the depot procured a hand trolley which was several feet above the ground but having wheeled it into place it was still not high enough. A pile of ashes nearby solved the problem, as we loaded the trolley with ashes until the desired height was reached.

Right, opposite page top left/top right: The importance of a Bothy at Backworth during winter time is absolute, not least when the bitter winter winds blow in from the North Sea some of the coal seams at this once extensive complex goes miles out under the North Sea.

Opposite page, bottom: Nassington, loco crew and shunter aboard one of the systems 16in 0-6-0Ts.

Top left/Bottom right: Brynlliw.

Top right: Castle Donington.

Bottom left: Shotton.

Pictorial Essays in Doubles.

Above: Austerity 2-8-0s in repose.

Right: Stanier 8Fs at Buxton.

Opposite page, top right: Stanier 8Fs in repose.

Opposite page, bottom left: Austerity 2-8-0s abandoned at Wakefield.

Opposite page, bottom right: Vacuum hoses at Crewe South on Tuesday, 17 October 1967.

Above: The digger on the EarlTree's ironstone branch, Corby, with Corby Iron and Steel Works in the background. Saturday, 30 November 1968.

Opposite: Studies inside Corby steel works featuring the Steel Division's Hawthorn Leslie/Robert Stephenson and Hawthorns 0-6-0STs with their distinctive yellow livery. Quite seperate from the mines divison they carried the ore from the pits.

The last survivor of Robert Stephenson and Hawthorn's powerful 18in 0-6-0STs at Backworth. These superb giants were more powerful than a Hunslet Austerity. No. 16 was the last survivor and is caught here pulling away from Eccles Colliery on the Backworth system. These 53 ton engines constituted one of the most powerful industrial types ever built in Britain and although these locomotives had to be given time when starting away with heavy loads, they very quickly dug their heels in and their massive free steaming boilers ensured excellent performance. At 85 per cent boiler pressure these monoliths developed a tractive effort in excess of 26,000lbs — higher than a main line ex LMS 4F 0-6-0.

Avonside of Bristol built this delightful 0-6-0ST in 1914. Named *Sir John*, the engine is seen here at Mountain Ash Colliery in South Wales.

British Leyland's Austin Motors car plant at Longbridge Birmingham had two of these giant Bagnall 0-6-0STs named *Victor* and *Vulcan*. Here *Victor* Bagnall No. 2996 of 1951 is at the head of a rake of cars from the production line at the exchange sidings with British Railways Wednesday, 5 January 1972.

Above: An unidentified Bulleid West Country Pacific races through the Hampshire countryside with an express for London Waterloo.

Right: Between the tunnels on Wishing Well Bank on the climb out of Weymouth, shrouded in smoke and steam, a British Railways Standard 5MT 4-6-0 climbs out of Weymouth with an express for London Waterloo. Express passenger steam continued on this main line until July 1967.

Opposite page: A Bulleid West Country Pacific bursts away from Bournemouth with a train for Weymouth. Re-built Southern Railway West Country Class Pacific No. 34034 *Honiton* heading away from Bournemouth with a Waterloo to Weymouth train.

Above: Peterborough sugar factory's Hudswell Clarke 0-6-0T hauls a rake of sugar beet into the factory.
This charming Hudswell Clark 0-6-0T played an important part in the creation of *Thomas the Tank Engine*.
Prior to preservation the engine was busily employed conveying wagon loads of sugar beet from the connection
with the main line railway to the sugar factory.

Opposite page, Top left: Lambton System. Top right: Peterborough sugar factory. Bottom left/right: Corby Minerals.

Opposite page, top left: Wennington Tunnel on the Carnforth to Settle line.

Opposite page, bottom: Climbing up Wishing Well Bank out of Weymouth.

Right: A Bournemouth to London Waterloo express speeds through Winchester, headed by Merchant Navy No. 35007 *Aberdeen Commonwealth*.

Below: A BR Standard 5 on the Bournemouth — Weymouth section.

Storefield's Andrew Barclay 0-4-0ST No. 19 caught at work in the quarry on 21 November 1968.

Top left: Storefield's Andrew Barclay 0-4-0ST No. 19 caught at work in the quarry on 21 November 1968.

Top right: Storefield Ironstone's 0-6-0ST No. 49 *Caerphilly*, ex-Stewarts and Lloyds Minerals, heads a loaded train through the wood cuttings on Thursday, 21 November 1968.

Left: Nassington Ironstone Mine's two Hunslet 16in 0-6-0STs *Jacks Green* and *Ring Haw* thread a loaded train through the Gullet in 1970.

Above: Leeds Holbeck.

Right: Patricroft shed.

Above: Patricroft shed cat with 8F No. 48467 on Saturday, 27 July 1968.

Left: Patricroft shed.

Detail studies of locomotives from the Scottish coalfield lying in Thomas Muir's scrapyard at Easter Balbeggie in Fife.
The two locomotives, top right, were built side by side at Andrew Barclay's Kilmarnock works as Nos. 2261/2 in 1949.
They had joint working lives on the NCB and amazingly ended up side by side in the scrapyard.

Above: Rebuilt Bulleid West Country Pacific *Dartmoor* arrives at Bournemouth with an express for London Waterloo.

Opposite page, top: A Waterloo train departs from Bournemouth behind BR Standard 5 No. 73029 on 10 December 1966.

Opposite page, bottom: The Bournemouth *Belle Pullman* service departs from Bournemouth in the semaphore signalling days of 1966.

Left: Solway Colliery at Moss Bay with their Hudswell Clarke 0-4-0ST No. 1814 of 1948.

Bottom: Hunslet Austerity at South Hetton.

Opposite page, top: Andrew Barclay 0-4-0ST at Penyvennie mine, Ayrshire.

Opposite page, bottom: Hunslet Austerity on the Cumberland coalfield.

113

Autumn in the New Forest. Re-built West Country Class 4-6-2 No. 34018 *Axminster*, caught near Beaulieu Road with the 12.32 Bournemouth to Waterloo train on Saturday, 22 October 1966.

Golden winter sunlight provides an evocative foil to West Country Pacific No. 34013 *Okehampton*, seen passing Mitcheldever with a Waterloo to Bournemouth express in the winter of 1966.

Merchant Navy in New Forest. Rebuilt Bulleid Merchant Navy Class Pacific No. 35008 *Blue Funnel* speeds westwards through the New Forest at the head of a Waterloo — Bournemouth express.

Left, bottom and opposite page, left: Hunslet Austerities with Giesl chimneys at work on the Cumberland coalfield. Part of the duty for these engines was to work the shale trains from the colliery out to the cliff tops for emptying in the sea below. It was a scenic and atmospheric location in which to enjoy trains in the industrial landscape.

opposite page, right: A Hunslet Austerity heads a rake of ladle wagons at Shilbottle Colliery, Northumberland. No. 45 a Hunslet Austerity built by Robert Stephenson & Hawthorns as their works number 7113 reverses internal wagons of shale onto the tip.

Sunlight, Smoke and Shadows: The sunlight filters through the blackened windows of the depot, mixing with the smoke and steam emanating from the engines inside. Maybe you can smell the soot, smell the oil and so glean something of the incredible atmosphere of these last cathedrals of steam.

One of the most famous and enchanting railway photographic locations was on the 1 in 75 climb from Tebay to Shap summit on the West Coast Main Line. A small stud of banking engines were allocated to Tebay shed to provide banking assistance whenever the driver of a northbound train felt he required it (great stigma was attached to any driver who failed to make the climb!). This beautiful area of England has sadly been disfigured by the M6 motorway but in Eric Treacy's time the tranquil days, clear air, gurgling becks and wild cries of the Curlew interspersed with the four cylinder throb of Stanier Pacifics. Shap was made famous by Eric Treacy who spent many happy days there when the line was 100 per cent steam worked and in so doing produced some of the finest railway photographs ever made.

Right/opposite page: Shap Bank as seen from High Scales Farm on Thursday, 28 September 1967.

Below: With the River Lune in the foreground, Standard BR Class 4 No. 75032 banks a north bound freight out of Tebay on the same day.

Islwyn, an Andrew Barclay 0-6-0ST drops its fire at the end of a working day at Talywain colliery, just north of Pontypool.

Whittle Colliery at Newton on the Moor operated this last surviving Robert Stephenson and Hawthorn 18in 0-6-0T No. 31. It became one of the most unpopular engines on the entire coalfield and was only bought out of store when serious motive power shortages occurred. Accidents including a rake of runaway wagons which hit the engine broadside caused chronic ailments, leaking boiler stays; and a fractured steam chest. One frustrated driver said "it's a race to get the work done before the engine empties its water all over the track, you can't see where you're going for leaking steam" — but this unhappy engine is loved by the camera see also title page. The rusty smokebox testifies to time in store. The high placement of spectacle glasses in the cab necessitated that drivers stand on wooden crates for a clear view ahead.

Stanier Black 5 No. 45342 heads a south bound freight along the West Coast Main Line south of Lancaster on Monday, 17 June 1968. This Black 5 was a Leicester engine for many years.

Scout Green signal box on Shap Bank
was made famous by EricTreacy who
regularly took tea with the signalman.

A BR standard 4 4-6-0 passes Scout
Green Signal box whilst banking a
heavy freight up Shap Bank.

Industrial contrasts at Polkemmet colliery in West Lanark in the form of No. 8 an Andrew Barclay 18in 0-6-0 saddle tank of 1900 and a standard Austerity 0-6-0 saddle tank of 1947 caught storming the gradient from the colliery up to Polkemmet Moor where the sidings and connections with the main line railway network were located. When this picture was made on a sunny morning in May 1972, the 72-year-old Barclay was the oldest working steam locomotive in Britain. Five loaded trains traversed the gradient each shift and these comprised of fourteen wagons holding some 600 tons of coal. Once a loaded train was ready, both engines were opened up on an all-out assault on the gradient. By positioning myself on the side of a huge slagtip I obtained a fine view of the bank and it was from here that the adjoining pictures were made. The Austerity created a steady even blast whilst the ancient lady in front weased and rasped away in a totally different rhythmic pattern so creating a marvellous polyphony of sound. Whilst watching these performances I was treated to a footplate trip on No. 8 from the colliery to the interchange sidings. Polkemmet Moor was situated amid slagtips in a wilderness setting speckled with industrial embroilment.

It was here that I met the celebrated railway photographer W. J. V. Anderson, his name being embossed on his camera case. 'What film stock are you using?' he demanded 'Agfa CT18 Reversal', I replied. 'That's no good here', he retorted in a rather haughty way. This place is colourless you'll achieve nothing with that stock here'.

I couldn't really argue with his view point; seldom had I witnessed such soot begrimed locomotives but I appreciated that the filth was an intrinsic part of the railway's mood and atmosphere, not least in this final twenty years of steam. I remember reflecting that, should any of Polkemmet's locomotives be preserved, and it seemed likely that one or two would — they should be retained for posterity in their begrimed apparel for the fascination of future generations. These were authentic musings, thinking of the ex-LMS 8F 2-8-0s allocated to Willesden where to find a clean one was like finding a four-leaf clover! Dirty engines were often described as being decked in Willesden grey but even more dramatic were the hundreds of Austerity 2-8-0s from the Second World War which never saw a cleaner's rag in their entire working lives.

The sun sets in the New Forest as a BR Standard 5 heads eastwards out of the setting sun bound for London, 1966.

The 20:28 Barrow to Huddersfield parcels train, headed by Black 5 No. 45310, crosses Arnside Viaduct against the blaze of the setting sun on Friday, 12 July 1968.

The Lambton System, County Durham.

Cumberland coalfield.

Left: Penrhiwceiber coal preparation plant, Glamorgan.

Below: Harrington Colliery, Cumberland. Note the vintage high visibility vest, a feature almost unknown at the time.

Right: Withdrawn locomotives at Trafford Park on 25 September 1967.

Right: Lostock Hall Depot on 20 September 1967. The obvious intention here was to frame the engine number in a chain-link but although the two lined up in the camera viewfinder, the image recorded was out of alignment with what the film saw. This problem with cameras in the 1960s was known as Parallax, of course today it could be corrected by computer but for authenticity I have left it as it was.

Far right: Abandoned ex-LNER Class B1 No. 61388 at Low Moor Depot, Bradford, as seen from the cab of an Austerity 2-8-0 on September 17 1967.

Withdrawn locos as Lostock Hall Depot on 20 September 1967.

Top: A Hunslet Austerity at work on the Cumbrian Coalfield.
Above, left and right: Hunslet Austerity working at Hafod rhy Nys
Colliery in South Wales.

A Hunslet Austerity makes its way through the valley at Hafod Colliery with a rake of wagons from the shale tip. A fall of snow has transformed the greyness of the valley floor into a shimmering white texture. Steam leaks from the ailing locomotive, waters cascade down the valley sides and the skies of South Wales seem perennially grey. A picture full of history as the world's first lcoomtovie was born in the adjacent valley

135

A pair of British Railways standard designs, the 9F 2-10-0 and BR Standard Class 4-6-0 abandoned at Carnforth after a short working life. All the BR Standard working designs were intended for mixed traffic work with the exception of these 9F heavy mineral class 2-10-0s, but paradoxically the 9Fs were so superbly balanced that they proved to be the best mixed traffic example of all the Standards and they began to be used on fast passenger schedules as well as heavy freight. Speeds of 90mph had been reported until this exciting but theoretically dangerous practice was forbidden.

A pair of ex-LMS Black 5 mixed traffic 4-6-0s wait to be towed to breakers yards as witness the cut motion for easy towing. A total of 842 of these highly capable locomotives were built between 1934 and 1951 — three years into BR. Few changes were made during their lifetime although some were converted with Caprotti Valve Gear and for many years these were allocated to Leeds Holbeck and Bristol. The Black 5s formed the basis for the later BR Standard 5s.

Running along the clifftops with a shale train; it is 11:00 at night and a Hunslet Austerity prepares to return to Whitehaven having discharged a rake of shale wagons.

Thomas Muir's scrapyard at Easter Balbeggie, Fife with right Grant Richie 0-4-0ST No. 61 works No. 272 of 1894 and left Andrew Barclay 0-4-0ST No. 22 works No. 1069 of 1906. Grant Richie and Andrew Barclay were both Kilmarnock locomotive builders, Tuesday, 4 April 1989.

A scene at Thomas Muir's scrapyard at Easter Balbeggie near Thornton, Fife, showing an Andrew Barclay 0-4-0ST, which had spent its working life on the Scottish coalfields. April 1989.

Thomas Muir's scrapyard near Thornton Fife with an Andrew Barclay 0-4-0ST No. 47 built in 1943 as works number 2157. Wednesday, 5 April 1989.

A walking dragline at work on the mines which surrounded the vast Corby Steelworks situated on the Northamptonshire ironstone bed.

An 18in 0-6-0ST taking water, Northamptonshire ironstone lines, 1970.

A Hunslet Austerity at work on the Northamptonshire ironstone bed. These sturdy 18in 0-6-0 saddle tanks worked on the minerals division of the ironstone network based in Corby. They were the largest engines in the fleet.

A Stanier Black 5 at Newton Heath depot during the final days of steam. In years gone by, this famous depot on the Oldham Road had a huge allocation of locomotives and was the birthplace of what became Manchester United Football Club.

Stanier Black 5 rumbles out of Newton Heath depot shortly before the end of steam.

Pulley w
depot a

Dense fog covered large areas of England on Monday, 29 November 1971 and here at Castle Donington Power Station a Robert Stephenson & Hawthorns 0-4-0ST has become isolated from its surroundings. The engine makes a fine contrast with the lineside hip berries, heightening the disparity between industry and nature.

With Drakelow Power Station in the background, Hunslet Austerity No. 1 passes *Progress* a Robert Stephenson & Hawthorns 0-6-0ST of 1946 in the colliery sidings at Cadley Hill near Burton on Trent. Cadley Hill was the last colliery in Britain to use steam traction.

Another rural scene featuring a Hunslet Austerity — this time in Scotland one of the NCB's Giesl-chimneyed variants is seen hauling a loaded train from the BR exchange to the Rexco plant at Saline.

Bournemouth Station was a wonderful place to see Bulleid Pacifics. It was a busy location, with continual flow of passengers augmented by rail enthusiasts from the late 1960s until the end of steam. The motive power depot was at the west end of the station and this combined with a friendly approach to visitors made Bournemouth a wonderful resort for rail fans. Sadly the locomotives became increasingly characterised by layers of dirt and the removal of nameplates, which were ever increasing in value.

One interesting engine was the Bournemouth Station pilot in the form of ex-LMS Ivatt 2-6-2.

Steam by night — Bournemouth Station in the dark hours. The Bulleids worked long distance trains from Weymouth to Waterloo serving Wareham, Poole, Bournemouth passing through the New Forest to Sorthampton, Eastleigh, Basingstoke, Woking and Waterloo.

The familiar silhouette of a Hunslet Austerity caught with a rake of loaded wagons at Shilbottle Colliery, Northumberland, January 1973. It was one of my favourite pictures, was made before turning professional but when I showed it to a friend, she said 'yes it's alright'. 'Alright'? I declared. 'It's more than alright' and I pointed out excitedly the symmetry of the two wagons and two trees; the golden winter light and the glorious tones of the yellow grasses in the foreground. 'Yes, I can see all that but there is still something missing' and upon pressing her further, she told me that there needed to be a magpie perched on the pole in the centre foreground and if the bird were there the picture would be a masterpiece, but without the magpie she didn't think so.

Of course she was absolutely right and it is impossible for anyone at Milepost to pick up or see this picture without smiling at the story of the missing bird. What my friend didn't know was that there were magpies flying around the coppice during the hour I waited for the train.

Stoke on Trent Motive Power Depot hosts a BR Standard 9F 2-10-0 in the summer of 1966.

Two ex-LMS Black 5s, no longer black at Crewe South shed on Tuesday, 17 October 1967.

One of Nassingtons inside-cylinder 0-6-0STs (left) in contrast with one of the Cranford ironstone system's outside cylinder 0-6-0ST from Bagnalls of Stafford (right).

Here is another superb example of the vibrancy between industry and nature in which the industry has ravaged the verdant surroundings and replaced them with aggressive shimmering gold ironstone and the gentle complementary colour of blue in the floodwaters below. Such contrasts make superb pictures too, like the abandoned machinery at Cranford or even the wild strawberries which grew in profusion alongside the rusty trackbeds. My time at Cranford was especially memorable as I was accompanied by the redoubtable Reverend Teddy Boston, one of the great figures in the story of railways.

Above: A line up of BR standard designs on Bournemouth motive power depot with an ex-LMS Ivatt 2-6-2T passing.

A Stanier 8F and BR Standard 5 4-6-0 at Patricroft in Manchester.

Weymouth motive power depot in the final months of Southern steam featuring a BR standard 4 2-6-0 and rebuilt Bulleid West County No. 34037 *Clovelly*, which had worked in from London Waterloo that morning.

A view along the boiler of a former War Department 2-8-0 No. 90406 in Wakefield loco shed, showing the injector feed, snifting valve and stubby cast iron chimney. During the 1950s some seventy-five of these War Department 2-8-0s were allocated to Wakefield.

One of the four named ex-LMS Stanier Black 5 4-6-0s on Patricroft shed Manchester. The locomotive is No. 45156 *Ayrshire Yeomanry*. Sunday, 9 May 1968.

A view from the smoke vents at Patricroft depot, Manchester, looking down on a Stanier 8F 2-8-0. Note the tender has been cleared of coal in readiness for the locomotive to be despatched to the breakers yard.

Llewellyn a Hunslet Austerity 0-6-0ST at work at Hafod Colliery on Monday, 26 February 1973.

Merthyr Vale Colliery Aberfan in mid-Glamorgan South Wales with No. 1 an 0-6-0T built by Andrew Barclay of Kilmarnock in 1953. In 1966 one of the colliery's slag tips collapsed on to part of Aberfan village killing 144 people, including 116 children who were in school and in the area, covered by the falling sludge. Tuesday, 21 December 1971.

Changing engines at Basingstoke with rebuilt West Country Class Pacific No. 34044 *Woolacombe* depicted here backing on to a York to Poole cross country train on the evening of Tuesday, 27 December 1966.

George Cohen's scrapyard at Cransley was located on the former ironstone branch from Kettering to Loddington. These scenes show ex-LMS Stanier Black 5s being broken up in the late 60s.

The end of steam on the Southern is highlighted by Salisbury BR Standard 5 4-6-0 No. 73093. This engine was broken up by Cashmores of Newport in March 1968, just a few months before steam ended on Britain's main lines.

PEN & SWORD
TRANSPORT

Published in 2015 by
Pen & Sword Transport
an imprint of
Pen & Sword Books Ltd
47 Church Street
Barnsley
South Yorkshire
S70 2AS

ISBN 978 0 90019 300 2

Typeset by Milepost 921/2
Milepost, Newton Harcourt, Leicestershire, LE8 9FH
Email: studio@railphotolibrary.com
www.railphotolibrary.com

Printed and bound in China by Imago Publishing Limited

Milepost 92 ½ would like to thank Calow Craddock Ltd for their assistance with the production of this volume

Pen & Sword Books Ltd incorporates the imprints of Pen & Sword
Archaeology, Atlas, Aviation, Battleground, Discovery, Family History, History, Maritime, Military, Naval, Politics, Railways, Select,
Transport, True Crime, and Fiction, Frontline Books, Leo Cooper, Praetorian Press, Seaforth Publishing and Wharncliffe.

For a complete list of Pen & Sword titles please contact
PEN & SWORD BOOKS LIMITED
47 Church Street, Barnsley, South Yorkshire, S70 2AS, England
E-mail: enquiries@pen-and-sword.co.uk
Website: www.pen-and-sword.co.uk